Running

FROM

PAIN

Denise L. DeLoach

Running From Pain

© 2025 Denise L. DeLoach

Winters Publishing
P.O. Box 501
Greensburg, IN 47240
812-663-4948
winterspublishing.com

To protect the privacy of certain individuals, their names and identifying details may have been changed and/or omitted.

Printed in the United States of America.

ISBN: 978-1-954116-33-7

In Memory Of:

Wallace DeLoach, my father
3/29/1946—6/17/2003

Linda DeLoach, my mother
8/01/1951—3/11/2018

MeLinda DeLoach, my sister
11/05/1968—4/27/2017

Acknowledgments

Thanks to:

Dan S.—From the Multiple Sclerosis Association of Seattle, Washington

Sarah James—From the Multiple Sclerosis Association of Seattle, Washington

All the Staff at St. Joseph Public Library in South Bend, Indiana for letting me use their computers to make a rough draft of my book. Special thanks to my friend Shannon Belecher at the library.

John Abernathy, my friend who is originally from Nashville, Tennessee, who encouraged me to publish my book.

Dennis Love, my friend from Anderson, for encouraging me to write this book.

Rayanna, my daughter who helped me with proofreading, the technical computer skills, and encouragement.

Winters Publishing, the publisher of my book.

Contents

Chapter 1

How I Grew Up

I grew up in South Bend, Indiana, a small town in the Midwest. I lived in a brick three-bedroom house, with a garage, basement, and a garden in the backyard. Our house was built from the ground up. My address was 228 Sheridan Street, on the lake side of town. My mother and father got married in the seventies, when Mother was twenty and my father was twenty-five years old. I grew up in a town where everyone knew you and your parents. I had two sisters named MeLinda and Shauntae DeLoach. They were also born in South Bend. My mother's name was Linda and her maiden name was Macturch. I have a half sister named Gina Battle, who was born and raised in Savannah, Georgia. Later, my father had a daughter named Brittany DeLoach. There were rumors that he had another daughter, but I am not sure. My late father was Wallace DeLoach. My mother was born in Mississippi, and my father was born in Georgia. My mother and father were together for nine years and married for fourteen years. My mother was the oldest of eleven children. Two children died at birth when my grandmother had them. My grandmother was married to my late grandfather, M. C. Macturch, who died in 1996. I have four uncles on my mother's side: Terry, Michael, Raymond, and Larry. I have four aunts, Dorothy, Joyce, Brenda, and Darlene. My father had a brother named Jimmy Ray DeLoach and stepbrother, Kenneth Wigfall. There are other family members who are not mentioned here. I did not know that my father was adopted until I became an adult, right before he passed away on June 17, 2003, at the age of 57 years.

My parents got married and their house was designed by my late father, Wallace DeLoach. The house had three bedrooms, with a bathroom, living room, and basement. We had a big front yard, and a big garden in the backyard. We also had an alley in the backyard of our house.

My mother worked at a factory named Nylon Craft in Mishawaka, Indiana, for 8 years. My dad worked at Eagle Products in Mishawaka, Indiana, for 15 years. They both had this factory work in common. My father also had his own business—moving, cleaning, and building cement driveways. They got married because my mom got pregnant with her first child and wanted to move out of her mother's house, but not because she was in love. She wanted to grow up fast because she did not have the freedom to do what she wanted to do as a teenager. My grandmother locked my mother out of the house if she was not in the house at a decent time.

I went to Harrison Elementary School for K–4th grade. My oldest sister, who was five years older than me, used to walk with me to school in below 0 temperatures, rain, sleet, and hot humid weather. My little sister, Shauntae, was 2 1/2 years younger than me. My oldest sister used to take me to school and pick up people along the way to go to school. My youngest sister was about two years old and went to my grandmother's house for daycare.

My big sister MeLinda and I used to get into fights. Our parents worked so much that my oldest sister used to help raise Shauntae and me. MeLinda used to babysit, cook, wash dishes, do laundry, and comb our hair, but it was a difficult relationship at times.

Our house never seemed to stay clean. I was about 8 years old then, and I had to clean up after two adults, two children, and myself. I had to wash dishes and pick up dead rats. Our house was so nasty and had a lot of rats, which was why I was scared to invite my friends over to the house. My bedroom was the cleanest room in the house. Our house had bunk beds, a dresser, and one kids' table and chair set. In the seventies, there were no PlayStations, cell phones, or computers given to children for their rooms. In the seventies, a bike was an important thing for a child to have, or a train set, or maybe a television for their room. I felt like a maid, growing up with my parents.

My mother was married but lived her life as a single mother without children. She was a working mother, but when the weekends came, she was often at the clubs. My late father was jealous because my mother liked going to clubs and not coming home at night. He often worked second shift and when he got home, my mother would be gone. My father did drink and my mother liked to party.

My late father was abusive, but my mother stayed with him and did not leave him. I told myself I would never date a man that drank and liked to party. I emotionally grew up with low self-esteem, because I heard and saw verbal and physical abuse. I thought I had a disability because I thought slowly. My parents did not pay attention to me as a child. They thought I was smart, but deep down inside I was a scared, miserable, and unhappy child. I was wishing for a full set of parents that showed me some type of love. I still wanted to ask God to please help me out of that situation.

My parents got a divorce when I was about 10 years old, and I was glad. I was tired of living in a rat-infested house, so we moved from that house to the projects. I was glad to move because I was scared of living in a messy house. I wanted to stay with my dad, but he wouldn't let me. My little sister was eight years old, and my oldest sister was fifteen. I knew it was God that got me out of that violence, dirt, and abusive situation.

About four years later, my oldest sister moved to Seattle. It meant fewer responsibilities of cleaning for me and less fighting with my sister. I had my own room, but my little sister was stealing my clothes from my room. She let her friends wear my clothes without my permission.

I turned seventeen and I had my first boyfriend named Terrell from Chicago. He bought me a ring with a heart shape, and I thought I was special. I was a virgin, and he did not know. About two or three weeks later, I went to his house with my little sister. He had a girl over and she had a knife. I could not believe my first boyfriend was just playing with me, and I learned early in life that men would always disappoint me. We were just teenagers, not adults. I was seventeen and Terrell was sixteen years old. When he was drunk, he did not know what was going on.

I was a senior in high school, and I wanted to go to the prom. I was working part-time at Kroger's and had to give my mother money to live with her. I hated the fact that I had to pay rent as a teenager. My mother depended on a welfare check for fifteen years. I saved enough money for my dress, shoes, hair, a purse, and a flower for my prom date, Remus. My Aunt Darlene let me borrow a necklace. My Aunt Brenda did my nails. My mother did not do anything for my prom. My dad let us drive his car. Neither of us had a driver's license, but Remus had a permit.

My boyfriend was seventeen, a junior, and a nerd. He did not buy me a flower, but he bought me a ticket to get in, dinner, and pictures. We went to one prom that had two different high schools, instead of going to two separate proms. After the prom, Remus asked me to pump gas, and I pumped gas all over my clothes. I had never pumped gas in a car, and I was embarrassed. I thought Remus should not have asked me to do that.

We went to a hotel, but our room was not reserved correctly. I accidentally locked the keys in the car when we parked, but I put my arm between the cracked open windows to unlock the door. My mother was waiting at the window for me when I got home at 5:00 a.m.

Then I met the security guard in our apartment complex. His

name was Michael. He was so fine. Michael was six years older than me. I was in love and did not care if my mother knew. I wasn't allowed to have a boyfriend or a male friend, but my little sister, Shauntae, could. It seemed she could do whatever she wanted, and she did not have to go to school. She was light skinned.

One night, Michael came over and it was late. My mother did not say anything and let me walk out the door. That night, Michael took me to the church parking lot down the street. He raped me and I tried to fight him, and I was a virgin. That night I called my friend Katrina and told her, because I did not know who to tell. I knew nobody would believe me. In high school, my parents thought I was having sex when I was not, because I wore tight dresses sometimes. My self- esteem was so low that I continued to have sex with him, because I thought that was what love was. I was only seventeen, and my parents did not show me a loving relationship. I was the outcast of the family.

I was eighteen when I graduated from high school, and it was the happiest day of my life. I finally got to escape that house, my mother, and my job at Kroger's, pushing carts. I got enough money from graduation to move out of my mother's house. I was planning to move in with my Aunt Joyce in Seattle, but at the last minute, she changed her mind. I was so desperate to move out because it seemed everyone was abusing my feelings and did not care. When

I was a child and until I was an adult, everyone called me "blackie" and "ugly."

When I was eighteen, I noticed my body was shaped up well and I had back pain. I was not fat, had no stomach, and weighed only 130 pounds. I could not talk to my mother, and felt I could not trust anyone. I didn't learn much from school, but just the basics like everyone else. I wish my parents could have trusted me and that I could have talked to them about anything.

Chapter 2

Leaving Home to Attend Seattle Central College

I was thick-skinned and knew how to deal with negative people. I knew how it was to be poor. I moved in with my older sister that used to fight with me. I needed a way out of the ghetto. Two weeks after I graduated high school, I moved to Seattle, Washington. When I graduated from high school, I had two suitcases and seventy dollars. I was going to have to get my hair done and buy groceries. I wrote my mother a strong letter because of the anger built up inside me.

I lived with my sister and my niece, and I wanted a way out of the hood. I took me three months to get a job at Jack in the Box in Seattle. I was happy to have a job. I met a man named Daniel, who was about ten years older than me. He was a customer who always came to eat lunch. Then I picked up a second job working at Safeway, being a courtesy clerk. I used to date him before I moved out of my sister's house. My sister helped me get some credit cards before I moved out.

One year later, I got my own place in downtown Seattle in a studio apartment. Daniel put his name on the lease with me because I had never had my own apartment before. He co-signed the apartment lease for me. My sister was mad because she was pregnant with her second child. I worked two jobs before signing up for school at Seattle Central College. I was nineteen and had only owned clothes. Daniel was never at the apartment, because he was an engineer that worked on boats. Daniel delivered food to different countries overseas and was home one weekend a month.

I was going to school for Cosmetology, but I was terrible at being a hairdresser. I switched to an Administrative Assistant major in college. My two-year relationship ended with Daniel, because it was a lonely relationship. He used to go to strip clubs with his friends and I got sick of him cheating on me. He used to bring me flowers every time he stayed out for two days, but he started being possessive towards me. I met a white girl that lived in my building and became friends with her and always spoke, but I never hung out with her. One day, when I came from school and work, my boyfriend had a messed-up bed, an unbuttoned shirt, and unzipped pants. This woman was sitting on my sofa with a T-shirt and boxers on. From that day on, I never cared about being faithful to a man anymore. I had many male friends. I talked on the phone with them, but I did not sleep with them. Daniel was the man I loved and wanted to spend my whole life with. I did love him, but not because he made $30.00 an hour, cheating on me in my face, and paying bills. I was working two part-time jobs and going to school full-time, and struggling. I had furniture, jewelry, and a gym membership from him, but I had to move on. I hated the fact that he used to force me to have sex with him and I did not want to be around him anymore. I was also verbally abused by my ex-boyfriend.

I decided I was too young for this mess and left my apartment in downtown Seattle. I decided to leave but moved to a bad neighborhood. I could afford to pay the bills and rent better because I was in school. I decided to move all my things out, and I did not tell my boyfriend. I got a restraining order on him, because he was violent towards me because I stopped loving him.

I had a larger, cheaper, and prettier place than my last apartment. And it was not a studio apartment, but a one-bedroom. The apartment complex had a park where children could play and an office where you could get computer skills. The neighborhood was mainly a Black neighborhood with nosy neighbors. The place had tight security because you had to sign in and out to come into the apartment complex.

I met a lady named Irea April, through my Aunt Joyce Macturch, who had also lived in Seattle in the past. My Aunt Joyce was a medical assistant who never came around much. My aunt gave me her number and Irea became my godmother. She used to braid my hair for $65. I met her in about 1992 in Seattle, Washington, and I came to her house to get my hair done.

My sister MeLinda lived down the street from my godmother Irea, with my two nieces, Elizabeth and Ellessea, in an apartment complex. They loved coming over for the park lunches in the summertime at my house down the street. One day, I was at the park playing with my niece Ellessea, because I had free time from work and school. I met a guy named Nathan. He was from Louisiana and went to Booker T. Washington High School. He wanted my phone number at a time when I was lonely, single, and available.

Nathan showed me the ropes in the bad neighborhood I lived in. He told me people got hurt. I was deeply in love but hardly knew him. I later found out he was a weed head, and everyone knew he was a weed junkie. I tried to help him with his résumé and encouraged him to get a job, but he did not care. He took care of his father who was sick, but his mother had died when he was young. He never got a chance to get to know her.

A year later, Nathan got paid by a government check to take care of his father. He stopped coming over to my house every day. That meant he did not care if we were a couple or not. His face started to sink in because he smoked so much. I continued to stay with him because no one else was interested in a broke college student. Four years went by, and I had just graduated from college with my two-year degree. I also got an office clerical certificate. My sister MeLinda and my godmother came to my graduation, and after the ceremony we went to Maya's, a Mexican restaurant in Seattle. Maya's was a very nice restaurant to get some good food and drinks, if you drank. I am not a drinker and that was the beginning of my escape from the ghetto again. I hated Seattle more than my hometown because the people were not friendly.

Three months later, I packed my bags and headed back to South Bend, Indiana. I felt I did not belong in Seattle. I got tired of struggling with low-paying jobs, meeting losers for men, and being depressed because of the rainy weather. I also got tired of riding the bus, and I was twenty-three years old. I had never had a license to drive or owned a car. I wanted to make my family proud of me for going to college, because I grew up in the projects, poor and with low esteem. I grew up with no sense of knowing if I was good at anything.

Chapter 3

Moving Back to Finish
My Bachelor's Degree

I moved back home in 1997, five years later, living with my mother and my little sister again. I moved home with my two-year degree in office clerical and $950.00 in cash. I thought I was rich, I had never had so much money at one time. I also transferred my job from Payless Shoe Source in Seattle, Washington. I was back in the projects again.

The next day, I had a welcome home dinner. My Uncle Larry gave me a dinner at my grandmother's house. My family was making up for five years. I was gone and they had not supported me in any way, except once a year, at Christmas time. The support that I got were gifts from my mom, dad, and grandmother, but from everyone else, nothing. I at least sent Christmas cards, but no gifts. I graduated from college, but no one cared, and my mother was disappointed in me. I met a man named Jesse at the party. And my sister started talking to our uncle's friend, Willie.

I was tired of living with my mother and sister and riding the bus to work every day. I decided to get my driver's permit but failed the test the first time by two points. The second time, I got my driving permit and passed well. I took my first driving lesson with my instructor and scheduled to take the test and failed. The second time, I passed, and it took me only five minutes, but the first time it took me about fifteen minutes to take the test.

I felt that Jesse was my first love as an adult. I had a few first loves as a teenager, but Jesse was different. He had my soul, body, and mind, because I would do whatever he wanted to do. I would even have a drink of wine with him.

I decided to buy my first car, which was a Buick Skylark. I finally got my driver's license, car insurance, and a car. I was so excited and felt a little free. I did not have to depend on the buses, my family at night or on weekends, and could come and go as I pleased. I worked at Payless for a few months at the mall and for about two years altogether. I was working 30–35 hours a week riding the bus, then suddenly, I bought a car and my manager cut my hours at work to 15–20 hours a week. They eventually hired another employee.

I decided to quit and worked at a nursing home as a dietary aide for three months. I met Tanya, who was my mom's friend's niece. Her uncle's name was Ronald, and he was dating my mom. I put one application in for Walgreens on Lincoln Way. It had just opened and I got hired. I was tired of low-paying jobs with a two-year degree. I decided to go back to school for my four-year degree. My parents told me not to go back to school, but they wouldn't tell me why. I did not understand why they said it. I disobeyed my parents because I was grown and didn't live with them. I got my own place again after nine months of living with my mother.

I worked at Walgreens for about a year, experiencing sexual harassment on the job. So, I transferred to the Roseland Walgreens and worked there for a year, then quit because I knew a new Walmart was being built. I broke up with Jesse because he pushed me off the porch, and I could have had broken bones. I couldn't deal with his heavy drinking and mood swings. He did something else that upset me.

I got an apartment, started school, and got a new job at

Walmart, and was doing okay for myself, considering I was very poor. And I came from a poor family. I made more money at Walmart than any job I had. I got hired as a cashier. I met a man named Ray at my cash register. He said, "Write this number down." I said, "You're crazy and I don't know you!" I waited a couple of days and called his number. I found out he was a truck driver. He had an apartment, his own car, and a job. I was very impressed that he did have those things.

We started dating and he would come over to my house on the weekends. I would sometimes stay over at his house on the weekends. He would cook me breakfast and have a barbeque for just the two of us. I met some of his family members. He told me about his family. His dad had twenty children and had been married twice. His family had their own church in South Bend, Indiana, but I had never visited it before. Both of his parents were decreased.

When we were dating, I was twenty-six and Ray was thirty-eight. He was twelve years older than me, but he lied about his age. He used to say he was ten years older than me. I usually don't like men more than ten years older than me. We fell in love, and I introduced him to some of my family members. We would go over to his brother's house to play cards. I introduced him to my dad, and he told me, "He is the one." I didn't know at first what he meant by that. Later, I understood that I would marry or have children by Ray.

One day, my dad said his stepdad was dying, and he needed to take a trip to Savannah, Georgia. I asked my dad, "Could I go with you?" He said, "Yeah." I asked my boyfriend Ray for some money to go on the trip. He didn't give me one penny, though I was his girlfriend. He was a professional truck driver, and he treated me like a dog. I knew he didn't love me. He just used me for sex. I was lonely, and no one else liked me at the time.

My father, his neighbor, Mr. Moody, and I drove to the South. We went to Register, Georgia in 2000. We went through mountains and rainstorms. I stayed awake for the long trip. I think it was a fourteen-hour trip. It was rainy and stormy the whole way.

When we got there, Mr. Moody took us to his family's house, and then we went to my cousin Mary Francis' house. This was my first time visiting my dad's side of my family as an adult. My cousin Mary Francis fixed us breakfast. We had grits with fresh peaches, Polish sausage, eggs, and juice. I couldn't eat all my food. My cousin Mary Francis said, "Baby, there're people in this world that are starving." I ate and she showed me my room. I decided to write a story about my trip for my English class for school. I was in college at Bethel College.

When I was there, I was introduced to my cousin Amy, who lived next door; she also cooked me breakfast. We had greens, pork chops, chicken, rice, and all kinds of food. I said, "This is breakfast!?" Amy said, "We eat off this food all day." There was cake too. It was red velvet.

The next day, we visit my grandfather in the hospital in Savannah, Georgia. He was nice and held on to my hand real hard. I met his wife too. We stayed a couple of hours. Then Mary Francis took us to Walmart in Statesboro, Georgia, and I used my discount card. We saw a street with our last name—DeLoach Street. There were a lot of businesses with my last name. I know there is a bottle of wine with my last name.

It was Thanksgiving Day, and we had a big dinner. We even had pecan pie with Mary Francis. Mary Francis and I picked the pecans from the tree. There were about seven of us and we had dinner together. The temperature was about 75 degrees outside. There was no snow, and it was Thanksgiving Day.

When I was there in Register, Georgia, I saw dirt roads, no sidewalks, cotton trees, and pecan trees. I picked pecans and brought them home. I also did my cousin's hair for free and for fun while in Georgia. I permed her hair, blow dried, and curled it. She liked that I had my hair braided, but she wanted me to perm her hair. She trusted me to do her hair, and I did a great job. I can do hair a little bit, but I don't enjoy doing hair.

We were ready to go a week later, and Grandpa was still alive. And I was glad. I didn't want to go to a funeral while I was there. It was fun. I wouldn't want to live there because it was too country for me, but the people were friendly and nice. On our way back home, we picked up Mr. Moody and went back to South Bend, Indiana. I had to go back to school and work. I had 6 months left to get my bachelor's degree.

When I got home, I found out that I had to repeat a statistics class. It was a math class I had failed in college, before I could get my degree. I had to get my degree in May and the degree paper would be missing. I had to come back in September 2001 to get my degree.

I was planning my party in advance because I had to pay for everything. I rented out the Carriage House apartment building for my graduation party in Mishawaka, Indiana. It was an apartment clubhouse. My mom cooked all the food. My dad and sister oversaw music. I had to cook two bags of chicken party wings myself, but my mom cooked a lot of food.

I went to Planned Parenthood in about March 2001 and found out I had pre-cancer of the cervical area. I never told anyone at the time, except my colleague Cynthia at school. I was a little scared because I had a boyfriend. I was cheating on him with a younger man, but he never knew. I knew he was cheating on me, so I didn't care. I just knew I was going to get better, even though I had the beginning stage of cancer. I was kind of suicidal, because I had a boyfriend that was treating me badly, not a great job, and I was not eating much because of lack of money. I had rent, a car note, an electric, gas, and telephone bill, and car insurance. It didn't leave much money for food. I had to go to the food bank. I was dating a professional truck driver, and he only gave me $20 cash over two years.

It was graduation day, and I cooked the chicken before graduation ceremony. I put on my gold dress and walked to get my degree. My mom wasn't there because she was cooking and being with her boyfriend, Paul. My dad was there, my little sister, my grandmother, and my Aunt Brenda. I still had pre-cancer, but I would soon get treated.

After I graduated, I had treatment for the pre-cancer with a 10-minute-long procedure where the doctor froze out the cancer. It didn't hurt at all. I felt better and I had a little more energy. I stopped talking to my friend Lawrence, the younger man I was cheating with. I stopped because I had to plan my trip out of South Bend to go back to Seattle. I kept working at Walmart for 45 hours a week, and registered for my last math class. I kept gaining weight and eating a lot, but I didn't understand why I was doing that. I started writing bad checks just to eat. I didn't want to, but I didn't have a choice. I didn't go to jail for it. I just paid extra fees later.

I finally decided that I was going to leave South Bend for the second time. I knew that I was running from the pain of being poor and never having a good-paying job. I didn't know what to do because I knew life wasn't going to get better. I was planning to finish my last class at Bethel, then quit my job, and move back to Seattle. I broke up with my boyfriend, Ray, but I kept letting him come back into my life. I even started counseling for a while. I knew that my life was going to get better moving back to Seattle again. I knew that God had a plan for my life.

It was December 2001, and I finally finished my last class. I shipped my car to Seattle and paid about $1,500. I didn't want to be there with no transportation. I took all the money I had and got a bus ticket. I decided to catch the Greyhound bus.

Chapter 4

Back to Seattle: Having My Child with Disabilities at the University of Washington

I caught the Greyhound bus and packed some food to go. I didn't have an appetite. Some lady on the way to Seattle brought me some food. I told her, "Thanks, but no thanks." I took the food, but didn't want it. I was depressed in a way. I didn't have much money, no job, and no sense of what I was going to do. I got to Seattle and some of my clothes were lost or stolen. I also lost pictures. I had bad luck and I had just gotten there. I didn't have a decent pair of shoes. I felt just like a bum.

My niece gave me a pair of shoes. I put my things in the back room. I slept on the couch and my godmother braided my hair for me. It was a couple of weeks until Christmas and I helped my godmother get things out of storage. I helped her decorate and put up her Christmas tree. I kept eating like a pig, I felt like I might have been pregnant. I wasn't sure because I had never been pregnant before. I left my godmother's house and decided to make a doctor's appointment. I made one for January, around my birthday. I was eating a lot, but I didn't have any other signs of being pregnant—no morning sickness.

It was January 28, 2002, and it was six days after my birthday. I had just turned twenty-eight years old. I took a pregnancy test. I was sitting down and a lady told me I was pregnant. I started to cry, and the lady said, "Why are you crying?" I said, "I just left my family from my hometown in South Bend, Indiana and have no job. I live with my sister." She said, "It will be okay because before you leave here, we will help you get yourself together."

The hospital assigned me a doctor. They took me back to the room and did an ultrasound. They gave me a picture of the baby that I couldn't really see, but which looked like a dot. They told me I was about two months pregnant. I was suicidal, but I didn't let the doctors know. I think the only reason I didn't kill myself was because I was pregnant. I was suicidal because I had debt, no job, no money, and no one to love me. I felt maybe God was trying to tell me this was a blessing in disguise.

I got prenatal pills before I left the office. The office signed me up for WIC checks, and another appointment with the clinic on Yesler Street at Harborview Hospital in Seattle, Washington. I walked out of the clinic to the right and signed up for a welfare check, food stamps, and medical coupons. That day, my whole life changed from being afraid to being motivated because I 'became a mother.' When I got home, my sister was more excited than I was. My nieces started to act out more than a little bit. I started to get sick, knowing I was having a baby and there was nowhere for us to live permanently. I got a temporary job for a couple of months working at a bank. I needed some money for diapers and some clothes.

My nieces started fighting and arguing with me when I babysat them. I gave my sister my welfare check money. It wasn't much, but I did. She charged $200–$300 a month. I bought food with my food stamps and WIC checks. I let my sister borrow my car sometimes. My godmother Irea would braid my hair for free because I didn't have any money.

I left and moved into a homeless shelter. I got tired of physically fighting one of my nieces. I didn't want to lose my baby. One of my nieces kicked me in my stomach. I went to go live in a shelter at the Aloha Inn in Seattle. It was a shelter for single men and women. My sister had asked me to leave, and I did. I had a room with a roommate and her name was Margaret.

I had to pay rent, but it was not much. I had to volunteer at the shelter too. I shared all the WIC food I got with the residents, because I did not have my own kitchen. Everyone in the shelter had an income, but I had to volunteer at the shelter and pay rent. I was there to work with released people who had just gotten out of jail or prison, ex-drug addicts, and ex-alcoholics. Everyone was genuinely nice. Also, the residents did not have any children.

The Aloha Inn board took me in when I had no place to go. A man brought me a necklace and some movies. He took back my movies because I would not sleep with him. He always kissed me and rubbed my feet for me. I could not sleep with anyone I hardly knew. I met a man named DeWayne, and he became my godbrother. He asked me to get on the board at the shelter. I said I would. I took parenting classes at the hospital in the shelter. When living in the shelter, you also must have a job, be looking for a job, taking classes, or going to alcohol or drug counseling.

I used to take my sister to work, and I was still living in the shelter. I tried to help her as much as I could, but it was never enough. Two days before the 4th of July, I drove myself straight to the hospital. The nurse said, "You're not going anywhere." I did not know what she meant by that. I felt like I was dying, and my baby was too. I was completely dizzy, could hardly work, and was scared. The doctors and nurses put my IV in and I could hardly breathe. The nurses keep testing my blood. At first, I didn't think anything about it. Then I realized they were testing me for drugs. I never did drugs in my life. The next day, a social worker named Diane talked about how she had adopted a mixed kid and married a black man. I did not understand why she told me that because my child was black. She was the director of social workers at the hospital.

The third day was the 4th of July, and I was on a strict diet. I would hardly eat anything. I had no ribs or tasty food. Nobody visited me on the holiday, and I was very lonely. I didn't get any calls while in the hospital. I thought my sister MeLinda and my godmother would call or come visit me on the 4th of July. None of my family in Indiana ever called about anything. That was nothing unusual for me. It was July 5, 2002, and Rayanna's heartbeat was getting low. That meant I was going to deliver my baby today. I was so worried, because I was alone with my baby inside of me with no family support, and it was an awful feeling. But I was going to be blessed like everyone else was. I was becoming a mother.

I called my only family that I had in Seattle, which was my sister, my two nieces, and my godmother to come to the hospital, because I was going to deliver my baby with an emergency C-section. I had eaten an apple earlier in the day and I couldn't breathe, so the nurse gave me oxygen. I felt like I was having a heart attack. Then I felt a little better, but I still felt like I was dying. It was getting dark, and I was getting more and more nervous, because I was scared my baby wasn't going to be okay.

The doctor told me my baby had turned around. I knew, and I kept it to myself that "God was here, and that my baby was God-gifted." I knew that my baby was going to be okay. But I knew that I was still under the weather. I didn't know for sure if I was going to live. I had magnesium in the IV in my hand the whole time that I was in the hospital. I wasn't eating much, and I was throwing food away in the trash and lying, saying, "I ate the food," because it was so terrible, with no seasoning. I just couldn't eat anything.

It was time for me to deliver and I could only have one adult in the room. I had to choose between my sister and my godmother. I chose my blood sister over my godmother. I had to choose because my baby and I were in a serious situation where anything could have happened. They put a needle in my back to help with the pain. Then I was in the room and the doctor started the operation. There was a screen that they put up where I couldn't see them operating.

The baby was born, and I had no idea someone was taking pictures. I saw my baby, and I held her for the first time and was in shock because she was so light-skinned. She looked like she was half-white. I knew who my baby daddy was, but I was thinking, *Wow, she's light*! I called her Rayanna Ebony. My baby was put in the ICU because she weighed 3 pounds when she was born. She had jaundice and that was why she was so light. She was a miracle child. She was a God-gifted child. I came out of surgery and my godmother went home. I felt like she was upset because I chose my sister over her.

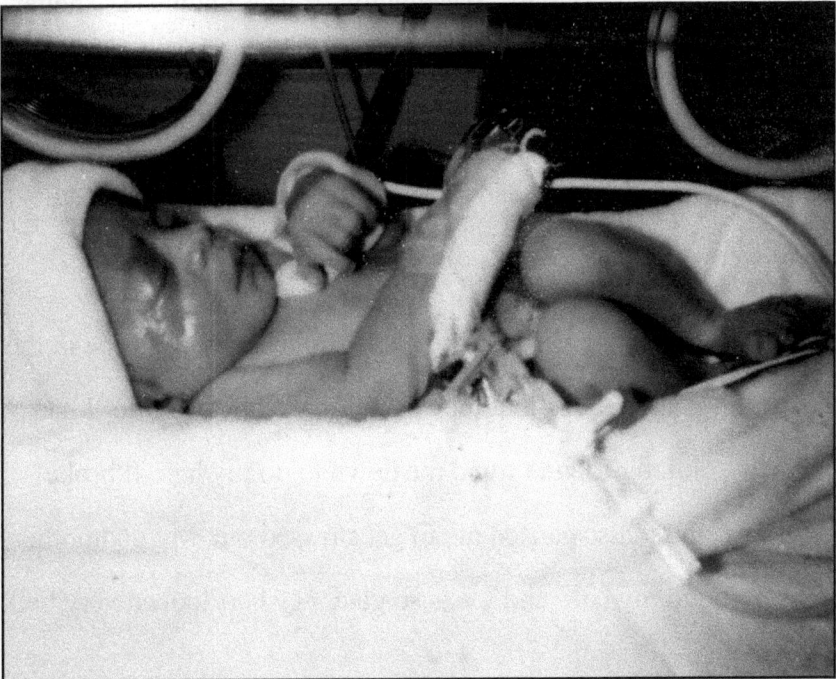

Rayanna Ebony weighed just 3 pounds at birth.

The next day, I had to eat more, use the bathroom, and move around. I was in so much pain and was very dizzy. I couldn't wash myself yet and take care of myself, but I got the strength to go see my baby in the NICU for newborns. I found out Diane had called CPS on me. CPS means Child Protective Services for neglected children. I found out she called because another social worker told me. Diane probably asked if I had other children on any report and I didn't. Rayanna was my first and only child. It was the first time I had ever been pregnant. I had preeclampsia, which used to be called toxemia. I had high blood pressure with fluids in my body. Another social worker named Heather came in to help me get into a house way out in Ballard, Washington. It was a homeless shelter for women with babies where you could live up to two years until you got yourself together. I was already living in a single women and single men shelter. I had to get ready to move out because there were no kids allowed.

About seven people from the Aloha Inn came to visit me in the hospital. I was shocked that they came. It was the day after I had my baby, and my friend turned me down to do my hair. It broke my heart, and it also caused me to get stressed out. My godmother came to braid my hair, and I was so glad. My hair looked very bad.

It was about the seventh day that I was in the hospital. My friend Marge from the homeless shelter caught the bus to pick me up from the hospital. We drove my car from the parking garage home. The hospital paid for my car to be in the garage all week. I was glad to get home. I knew it was the shelter, but it had been home for me for almost 2 months. I left the hospital with 8 pills because I needed to control my blood pressure. I kept visiting my baby every day at the hospital. I was there all day and every day to see my baby. I would catch a cab every day to the hospital. I also breastfed my baby. I pumped milk, but a lot did not come out. I did not think I could feed my baby because when I was about twenty-three, I had a breast reduction. But I knew God was here in my life. I had an angel on my shoulders. I drank herbal tea that my sister's neighbor gave me to produce extra milk.

On Friday, July 12, 2002, at approximately 3:30 p.m., I came into the NICU and asked a nurse if she would care for my baby. She responded with an 'attitude,' stating that she had just come on her shift at 3:00 p.m. I left at 4:00 p.m. to go pump breast milk in the room down the hall. About 15 minutes later, I returned to the NICU and found out that Rayanna's monitor was beeping; she was red, crying, and screaming. Rayanna's face was buried in the blankets, and she was suffocating. The nurse was attending to other babies in the NICU and ignoring Rayanna. I got upset and stated that nobody was watching Rayanna. Then the nurse, Susan, came over to look at Rayanna, She walked away and left to address another baby. I turned Rayanna over, calmed her down, and put a pacifier in my baby's mouth. I checked her temperature, changed her Pamper, and fed her. While I was feeding Rayanna, my sister, my two nieces, and her friend came to visit. I left Rayanna at 5:45 p.m. to pump breast milk. I came back at 6:00 p.m., but could not find the nurse to put the milk in the refrigerator.

The nurse who was supposed to be attending Rayanna was not around. Nurses kept making comments about me in the hospital. The nurses made comments like:

"Where do you live?"

"Is your baby's father a drunk?"

"Did you braid your own hair?"

"My baby is mixed race too."

"Do you have your own car?"

"Do you have your own room?"

Marsha (a Black social worker) had told them that I lived in a shelter. I did not tell anyone because I knew the doctors and nurses would call CPS on me because I was Black, homeless, poor, and a single mother.

I talked to Doctor Levy about this matter. I told him that I was tired of the nurses asking me personal questions pertaining to my daughter and me like: "Where do I live?" or different questions all day and everyday for two-and-a-half weeks. The nurses had no respect for me and the confidentiality law. The hospital staff acted like I was dumb and stupid, like I was a teenager. I was a human being, a college graduate, and almost thirty. I was twenty-eight at that time.

Dr. Levy told me that during a meeting with the social workers and nurses, Diane told everyone that I lived at the homeless shelter and did not have a place for Rayanna to go. He also said, "That the nurses do not like you." I told him that I was not here for them to like me, but to make sure my child got proper and appropriate medical attention. I wrote this incident report to the health department. I also wrote some positive comments in my daughter's medical reports about my behavior. I was not found with drugs or alcohol, or guilty of prostitution. They also called CPS to see if I had other children; but I didn't, this was my first and only child. The hospital also put in the medical reports that my daughter was mixed race and she wasn't. I went to human rights, and they did nothing. The hospital finally wrote me about 14 letters apologizing for their behavior. But the hospital did put me in the system— when Rayanna had a place to stay. We didn't have our own house, though.

I left the Aloha Inn and moved into another shelter for eight women and their children for one weekend, then left. Two-and-a-half weeks later, Rayanna left with my sister and my two nieces for about two months. Then I went to live in another shelter which was an apartment building. It was transitional for two years. I was there for two months, then finally got public housing. I stayed with my sister for six months and was homeless for about four-and-a-half months.

I got public housing and stayed there for one year. I signed up for Section 8 housing with a lottery and it took 18 months. It took a while, but we finally got a nicer apartment. I also had to take a DNA test for Rayanna and the test came back 99.99%. My baby father requested it from Indiana. We took the test at the Seattle County–City Building.

I finally got my child support check 18 months after my daughter was born. I got off welfare and was getting child support, food stamps, and medical coupons. I took the money and paid some bills, and we saved money to get out of Seattle. The CPS people were following Rayanna and I around. I hated that feeling. The system wanted my baby, and I didn't have a drug or alcohol problem. I was so depressed and I couldn't find a lawyer to sue the hospital. I shouldn't have been working, but instead, be financially well off. My life was ruined and the social workers who messed my life up were still working, and they should have been fired. The social worker at the hospital made false statements and ruined a lot of women's lives. Seattle used to be a beautiful place to live, but if you have Black children, forget about it. That is just my opinion.

I even signed up to be a paralegal at a community college. I took classes and they were paid for, but I dropped out because I had surgery. I got my gallbladder taken out. I just was tired of catching the bus, and I felt I wasn't very good with computers and writing because my nerves were bad. I almost had a stroke in the hospital, then I had my daughter, almost died, and CPS was trying to take my baby. How could I study? I did not have any family support. I had just gotten child support and then they told me I had to pay the money back. I had to pay the money back to the welfare office.

I moved back home about three years later. The baby and I caught the train home. It took us two days to get home. I finally was free from the pain of CPS following me around. I had three places that were harassing me: CPS, the child support office, and the welfare office that were trying to make me feel bad about myself because I had my first and only child. I almost lost my mind, but I didn't. God saved me from losing my mind, because I was a Black single mother who wasn't working at the time.

Chapter 5

An Injury to My Wrist

Rayanna and I arrived at the train station and my mother picked us up. She was late, but it was still light outside. I was disappointed that my little sister and my nephew weren't there or any other family members. Rayanna was two years old. And she been on a train, plane, and the Greyhound bus. So, Rayanna and I wanted to help my mother out and she could help me. It was September 3, 2004. My mother let Rayanna and I stay with her for three weeks and I did what I could to make sure we wouldn't come back to her house. God gave me a second chance because Seattle was a terrible experience. I did not want to live there ever again.

We moved to Indian Springs Apartments and I had to put down a $250 deposit. I had eight boxes shipped over to my best friend,

LaTanya. My mother and sister would not let me ship things to their house. My mother let me borrow three lawn chairs and a small 12-inch television. It was not a flat screen television. Our apartment was nice and clean. It was a decent neighborhood. We lived there towards the end of September 2004. I bought a used mattress and box spring from a warehouse on Portage Street. We slept on the mattress and box spring on the floor, but we were at home.

My sister told me about the REAL Services self-sufficient program. My case manager's name was Jane Wright. She told me about different programs like First Steps. The First Steps program worked with special needs children or premature children. She helped me get Rayanna into school at 3½ years old and she helped me get her into speech therapy. She gave me a referral to get clothes and furniture for my apartment. She even helped Rayanna get social security, but it was not much. It helped us, because I was not working yet. She saved my life. I even went to counseling.

I got a job as a temporary secretary at South Bend School Corporation in the special education department. I only worked two weeks. Then, I finally got a job as a substitute teacher. My daughter was in Head Start. I got voted in as a vice-president on the Head Start board. We did not get paid, but it was fun going to meetings. I was a volunteer at her school. We went to San Antonio,

Texas for a conference.

One day, I came down my stairs with Rayanna in my arms from my upstairs apartment. I tried to walk across black ice and fell on my right wrist and broke it. I was embarrassed and scared someone was watching us. I got up and took Rayanna to school because she had missed the bus. It was February 7, 2007. I went to work later that day and had to put on a wrist brace. Three days after my accident, my hand and wrist turned blue and black. After work, Rayanna and I went to Saint Joseph Hospital and sat there for three hours, before we walked out. I went to Memorial Hospital, and I was crying and my blood pressure was out of control. They wrapped my arm and wrist up.

The next day, the emergency room at Memorial Hospital called and said, "We made a mistake and you have more broken bones than we thought." At first, they had told me that I had only one broken bone in my wrist. The hospital referred me to a doctor at Edison Lakes.

I got my wrist cast taken off. Then my new doctor at Edison Lakes put me in another cast. I went back to work with my second cast. My cast was removed eight weeks later. The doctors said, "Your bones didn't heal right. We don't have to do surgery." I said, "I need a second opinion." He referred me to Dr. Randy Felic at

South Bend Orthopedics.

I went to see Dr. Randy Felic and found out he is the son. His father is a doctor too. Dr. Felic had X-rays done on my wrist. He came in and said, "Denise, you're in bad shape." I said, "I've been

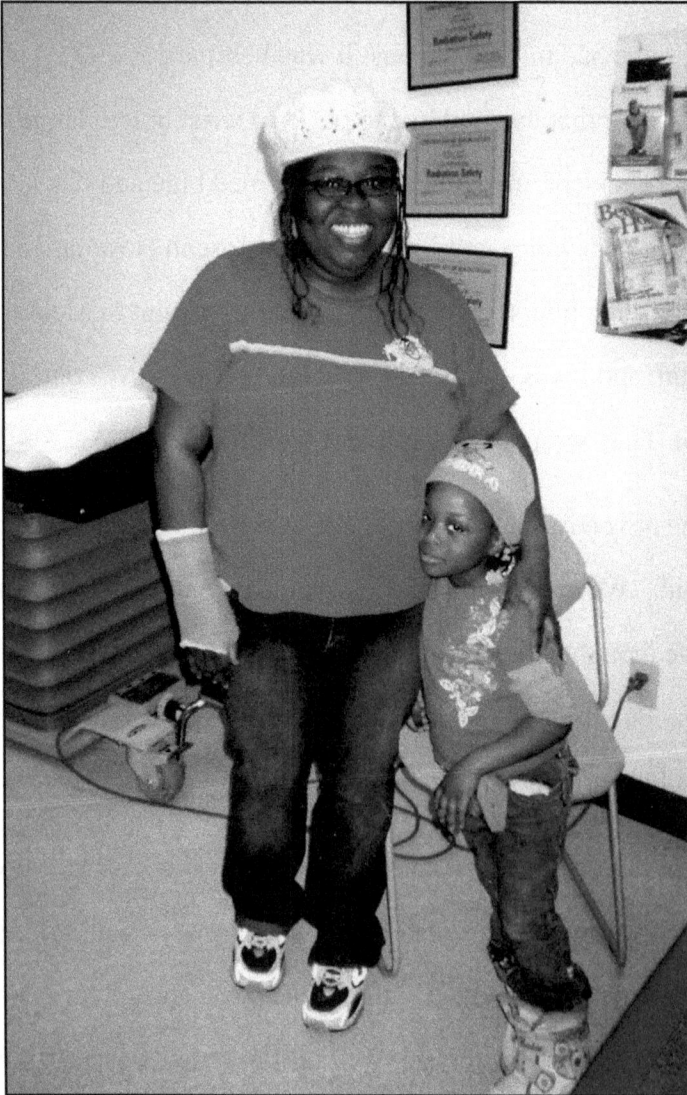

Denise and Rayanna.

in the hospital, at Edison Lakes Clinic, and now I'm here." He said, "You have a bone disease called Kienböck's disease." He told me that I needed surgery, and if I didn't have surgery, I wouldn't be able to use my wrist or arm again. The doctor had to take three bones out of my wrist. I called around to get a lawyer. The lawyer helped me get medical records and it was about two hundred and fifty dollars. My lawyer fired himself because he said I had a pre-existing condition. I had no choice at this point about what to do. I went to small claims court to sue my apartment complex, but didn't win.

I didn't know what to do because my wrist was messed up for life. I decided to ask my apartment complex if I could move to a downstairs apartment because of my accident. The lady downstairs complained that we were too loud anyway. The landlord accommodated me and let me move downstairs to an apartment at the back of the complex.

I decided to have surgery on January 2, 2008, almost a year later. I got laid off my job and was getting unemployment for four months. I had surgery at Saint Joseph Hospital and I was a charity case. After surgery, I was tired and hurt. My uncle came and picked me up at the door and drove me to my car in the parking lot. I drove with one hand to pick up my daughter from my mom's house. Then I picked up my pain medication. After that I drove to get a cart full of groceries at ALDI's. A cashier there helped me

pack my groceries; she was very nice and helpful. At the time, it

was cold and snow was everywhere. God gave me the strength to

do all that.

Chapter 6

A Successful Homeowner

After my accident, I got a job at Penn–Harris–Madison School Corporation, working part-time in the kitchen. I didn't go to work in South Bend, Indiana anymore. I went to sign up with Habitat for Humanity and got an application. I got denied the first time. I reapplied and got more income coming in. I got accepted into the program. I took classes, volunteered at people's homes, and worked on building my own home.

I was in the program for eighteen months and I became a homeowner through Habitat for Humanity. I had the fourth biggest and prettiest house in my family. I went from homeless to a brand-new home built from the ground up. God loved my daughter Rayanna and me more than I loved myself. God took care of me when I was poor and single and when I was trying to get out of the hood and out of poverty. God never left me when I was down.

I was thirty-six years old when I got my first home with Habitat for Humanity. I was single and worked at the school corporation as a lunch lady and a substitute teacher. It was a beautiful blessing to be a homeowner, even though I wasn't rich. I had beautiful memories there and some bad ones. I will be working on a part two to this book with memories in the beautiful home where I used to live in South Bend, Indiana. I currently live in southern Indiana. I was married to my beautiful house for almost 10 years. The second book will talk about my experiences living in my Habitat house.

❧ **About the Author** ❧

Denise L. DeLoach was born in South Bend, Indiana, in 1974. She currently works at a hospital and sells Mary Kay. She is living in southern Michigan. She is a first-time book author.

Deloach is a high school graduate of James Whitcomb Riley High School in June 1992. She graduated from Seattle Central Community College with an Office Clerical Certificate and a two-year degree as an Administrative Assistant in 1997. She also graduated from Bethel College with a Bachelor of Science degree in organizational management in the College of Liberal Arts in December 2001. She continued her education at Ivy Tech Community College in Muncie, Indiana with a Certificate in Paralegal Studies and a Technical Certificate in Paralegal Studies in December 2022. Deloach also has a Certificate as an Electrocardiography Technician from Marion, Indiana's Ivy Tech Campus and a Technical Certificate in Healthcare Specialist. She has never been married. She has one daughter, but she helped raise her two nieces when they were younger. She wants to continue writing nonfiction memoirs that are inspirational.

When her daughter was four years old, DeLoach was voted

in by parents to be a vice-president of the Head Start class. She worked for South Bend Community School Corporation as a substitute secretary for two weeks and a substitute teacher for a year. She worked for Penn–Harris–Madison School Corporation off and on for twelve years as a bus aide (for a couple of months), a food service worker, and a substitute teacher. She also worked for Anderson School Corporation off and on for four years as a paraprofessional teacher, substitute teacher, and a food service worker. DeLoach worked for the school corporations for about seventeen years. She worked all her life doing home care, sometimes paid, but most of the time unpaid.

Her hope is that this book helps others to know they aren't alone when it comes to trauma. Believe in the Lord, and always pray that He will help you when there are hard times. This book was therapeutic for her to write and she hopes it will help you too.